A PUBLIC WOMAN

∀

PUBLIC
WOMAN

BENNO BARNARD

EYEWEAR PUBLISHING

TRANSLATED BY DAVID COLMER

NEW AND SELECTED POEMS

First published in 2015
by Eyewear Publishing Ltd
74 Leith Mansions, Grantully Road
London W9 1LJ
United Kingdom

Typeset with graphic design by Edwin Smet
Author photograph Renata Bakker
Printed in England by TJ International Ltd, Padstow, Cornwall

This book was published with the support of the Dutch Foundation for Literature.

Nederlands
N letterenfonds
dutch foundation
for literature

MIX
Paper from
responsible sources
FSC
www.fsc.org FSC® C013056

*Eyewear wishes to thank Jonathan Wonham for his very generous patronage of our press;
as well as our other patrons and investors who wish to remain anonymous.*

WWW.EYEWEARPUBLISHING.COM

BENNO BARNARD
(born 1954) has lived in Holland,
England, Belgium, Spain and the USA, where
he taught literature at the University of Texas.
The winner of several important literary prizes,
he has published some twenty books and
has also translated Auden, Celan and
many other poets into Dutch.

DAVID COLMER
is an Australian translator of
Dutch literature. He has won several
major prizes. In 2014, *Even Now*, his selection
of the poetry of Hugo Claus, was shortlisted
for the PEN Award for Poetry
in Translation.

Table of Contents

The Castaway

A Kiss in Brussels

We stand here freezing in our winter coats,
a kiss prevents my breath from showing white,
my hand slows to a halt in mid caress,
I want to let you go, but not tonight –
my fingers in your hair, the evidence.
Here for a second in this city park,
we're two cold lovers mouthing March,
who kiss as though exchanging quotes.

Mother Tongue

In memoriam Christina van Malde, 1919–1995

Your features are white like the milk
I drank in the house on the Amstel
where I was born. (Sure, Paris in spring
was a good fit, but summer swelled and burst
your two-piece suit and by November
rain and twilight filled the pane: a pale,
nineteenth-century hand descended
on my life.) Mama, I know full well,
I was an angry flower blushing pink,
I haven't changed. I'm too much, too little, too Dutch.
And my big mouth still sucks
on the consonant that tasted best.
Even now my oldest vowel is all amazement
at my greed and my contentment.
Milk-fed my whole life long.

You remind me of things I've never known.
You make up rhymes, like before, with animals and nonsense words.
Today you were my governess with the rod:
today we did morality, causality,
the flight of birds and a touch of God.

It was only here in Antwerp I started loving you,
like a fiancée with blue black eyes
and the heart of a lion. Often you sit at the bar
babbling on, but with your naked legs wrapped tight
to protect your little predator... I swallow
your diphthongs like hosts and call you love,
because someone has to call you that and mean it;
I take you home with me and in my sleep I hear your heels,
awkward on the gleaming honeycomb of cobblestones.

My father-to-be called you Katinka Maldovski.
You are my mother who doesn't listen to me,
but talks up a storm in my teacup.
Now you are gone through a hole in the budding earth
and tomorrow is another night
for me to write:

I'm not just mine.

Dream of 1968

We were in our old house, the two of us.
Paris was burning in hundreds of fires:
ash from a hecatomb of smouldering tyres
came drifting over woods and overhead

and through that spring until a farther north.
For Prague would shortly fall, that much I knew.
Soon I would speak my first dissenting words –
soon I would sit unheard in this blind spot

to chant my epic Homer. Suddenly
that unfamiliar voice above your book:
'There's nothing you can do. Just go away.'

The cuckoo clock calls onomatopoeias
and drowns you out, father, but I still name
your name in all the prayers I never say.

Aubade

For Piet Piryns

We talk until we see the morning double.
The bar is spinning from the cigarettes.
A dishcloth on the tap is wrung and sleepy.
'If I knew who I was, I wouldn't be me.'

We make our way straight-backed to the toilet.
Ah, l'orgasme du pauvre… The river runs dry.
The front door yawns about the morning paper.
Another man is aping death.

Ah, friendship's demented reign of terror!
Few dare to raise their voice against the heavens,
many will see the sparrow fall and not reach out their arms
(although the barmaid with the dimples has her charms).
We'll take our knives to the wind that blows her harm!

And now we've nothing else to do, let's raise a hollow glass to
      the mothers
we bury deeper and deeper in the iron anecdotes of childhood,
remembering with a smile that wasted longing for a South
beneath the silver clouds, iconostasis of these misty lands…
And to our fathers, murdered so much more than necessary!

'I've written a book, but haven't read it.'
'No one told us who we were.'
We scrape our hearts out till they're empty.
We mumble like Jews.

The day is white as dough.
I stare with stinging eyes
at the gods' gold watch,
hung between the fraying clouds:

the time is three thousand years in Europe.

New Year

Was it a rumour, like death's a rumour
at sixteen? A knife that slices someone open? Someone?
The old lady, maybe, in the Grand Bazaar,
shuffling thin-lipped to the checkout,
to settle an enormous debt. Angel hair
burning suddenly on anachronistic shoulders.
Or the man in the bar with his tainted brain,
perhaps. In the end beer will out,
nonsense spouting from his nicotined mouth, spit
spraying on my shirt. 'If only I didn't stink like this…'
Or yet another, lonesome on the TV show
SO THIS IS LOVE? (the spotlights make the shining armour).
He was a contestant, no one fell
at his first and only sight. I felt a tinge of pity, yes.

All this flashed through my mind like a knife,
startling last summer's butterflies, shimmering,
rustling autumn leaves, meaning nothing, causing no damage either:
because I, after all, was not one of them, I was my words

and I had used my time as if it were a condom.

And you, hostess with the mostest pouring the night away
at the bash we had! It lasted till next year:
the moment came with frothy cheer
and my thoughts bubbled, I proposed a bubbly toast…
but most of what I said I felt no urge to say.
My tongue was wagging at the stars
from where I, as a child, had sprung.
Your empty glass snapped laughing from its stem.

What makes me so restless? Is it a warning, a dream?
But aren't the past and future both unreal?

I thought they were. And did I spurn love,
didn't I bare my heart, didn't I bury my mother in your year?

I just can't tell, not talking to a soul.

The Poets

We,
sightless voyeurs under the petticoats
of the heavens,
deaf philosophers scratching away
at violins,
living authorities on our death –
we are mad with desire

for you,

but have nothing but froth
under skirts, catgut art,
pointless evocations of great
mysteries;
our desire lacks an all-
encompassing music.

'Narrative! Narrative!' you cry.

And so there's love and death:
someone strings an impossible bow;
another assumes the cloak of madness
to avenge his begetter,
in middle age the third looks up
in the old chaos of the sun.

We've held out till now,
because, despite it all, the anecdote
needs the sublime and the sublime,
the anecdote. Forgive us our pitiful
fiddling with commas and colons.

In the hope that the wind will blow through our work
we write our lovesick poems

for you.

Shul

On the wall of a former synagogue

Passer-by, this was a house of prayer
for nonzealous believers:
Salomon Samuel Frank, shopkeeper,
Nathan Jakob, of honest conduct,
name them. Here
they gathered: instructed
by forefathers, borne
by tradition.

Realise:
there is no such thing
as a former shul.

Think of the bastard who stored
his winter potatoes inside.
It is not nothingness
that terrifies
but its revelation in banality.

Even now, a cold millennium later,
an old man still stands
under the eternal lamp
mumbling in all his unshavenness
at the ark containing the names
of people death
scooped up like so many spuds:
Sam, Israel, Esther, Benjamin, Jakob.

You who are a passer-by,
as they were,
name them.

Moving House

The boxes for crisps and bananas
are packed with the bric-à-brac
of human memory:
plugs, artefacts, burial objects –
relics,

gradually grown cultic
from perishing in the attic,
and now being relocated.
Carved bones, painted shards
to protect our fleeting souls
from almighties and telluric forces.
We are hunters and gatherers.
We are fleeing Trojans,
nine cellars behind us.

Is that a thought?
But every thought is a frantic game
of dice on the cart now jolting
out of Asia Minor,
followed by the neighbour's Rottweiler
and some Hector's bouncing body.

One plate goes to the gods.
Inside a box – unseen, unheard –
the wooden alphabet
spells a word.

Where there's a will, there's the West.

It's not until we arrange our bed
between new walls, locate power points,
and check the immeasurable space
in every box of books, that we
relax as people of the modern age.

The Golden Boy

The woman I'd wedded pushed hard against death.
He wasn't yet able to wade through the stream,
wasn't yet able to clamber up rock,
his way led him head-first from unborn to here,

where myth gives suck with leaking tits
and heroes jostle like thirsty stock
around the magic trough,
TV.

She needed no gods, no snake oil:
she worked hard in a private tug of war,
twisting, as if around a cue.
Big was the head of that kid.

Until I saw his ear, the unexpected ear –
without a Down's fold, you see –
it struck me dumb as if I'd lost a bet
or caught an errant eight ball in my mouth.

Now (he's just turned two and so)
he needs heroic deeds and hurls
himself, a frothing blond cascade,
across the hall and up the stairs at Dad.

Last night, while rinsing off shampoo,
I stopped and stared at the top of his head,
his hair that swirls like disappearing water,
and thought, *What am I putting you through.*

Flesh Relations

In the slow campaign
of day to day
they fall.
Four grandparents begat us and died,
followed by uncle, uncle, aunt

and then the first parent,
the first friend, the enormous news
of someone else's run-down kid –
flesh relations one and all.

Braying down the iron road
from Plato to Hollywood,
Brother Donkey breathes his last.

Sometimes we see their backs. Sitting down
before our squinting, dazzled eyes or shuffling past
with shopping bags. Strange reincarnations:
her, white as snow in a raincoat; him, turtle bald,
with shoulders like a hopping bird's.
Antilight was playing tricks.
Their return is shocking and no consolation.

They're nowhere to be found on the winter's day
that bleeds to death along the river –
they are not in nature, not in a butterfly
reminding us of psyche, the wind
doesn't mention their names. And all you find
in the streets of the world, its settlements
and cities are associations.

They do appear occasionally in dreams
(those foolish wicks in the unfathomable):
bending over us with searching eyes,
then leaving us behind.

The Lake Inside of Me

The lake inside of me flows from another lake
that's down below. They're not of equal size.
My lake's a word and of a different depth.
It's deep enough to drown, but no one dies.

Can origins be interchanged? The waters rise
and fall, but equally; the source that feeds the sea
is fed and to the same degree. There is no fountainhead.
Eternity's a river – constant motion – in between.

My lake is not below. Below, the sun reflects,
the dazzlement of all I've known. Your name,
written in water, is valid all the same.

Prithivi the Dentist

Behind the hedge of his teeth he waits
for the ivory fingers that gleam on all
her many hands, full of moonlight.

Fireflies and water nymphs attend her,
hobgoblin owls and godly sons –
nerves jangle, this lady's demonic!

A thunderstorm rolls over the shrinking fields.
The mine delves its dismal passion.
A team of horses dances down the path.

Mercy, his thoughts cry out in chorus;
and her eyes are full of snow-white vistas;
brooks babble down the mountainsides,

the gurgling water laughs away his fear.
The coals have been quenched in the valley
and the sun cools off before his eyes.

Now the silence waits for a piano:
the floor has been polished, the mouse hole tidied;
a gentle roof arches over the two of them –

and beckoning ahead of Goldentongue:
the leg of lamb, the art of threading words
and, from his love, a hot French kiss.

The Rat

Living on a scat-strewn wasteland,
surrounded by steel bars. Darkly chewing
on cheese rinds, Biblical passages, the origin

of species; gnawing – with thunder in your skull –
at the moon and the shadow of the piano
(when the human female plays by candlelight:

the sea crashing on the rocks, the winds of autumn
crackling in a chestnut row, a solar storm
raging in the province of a greater world

where armies never came). And sleeping. Waiting
for children's hands. Racing, racing a little
in your wheel. Feeling lonely and neglected.

But scratching with your claws, tightrope walking
with your naked tail, juggling giant balls, vibrating
your nervy whiskers, you, grey velvet, arouse disgust.

Housewives, forget Hamelin, forget the sewers,
the buboes, the powerless barber-surgeons,
the rhythmic splash of oars in black water.

Love Merlin. He knew Arthur at Camelot
and here, perched on the shoulder
of the crown prince, he still reads along.

The Traffic Jam

Hurrying slowly home over rock-
hard earth. Life itself descends to the sea
in an even slower cascade: a year

makes the edge, tips, falls and breaks on the ledge
below. The mountain is romantically forested
but rolls you down like a living stone:

you roll and roll, no way to gather moss.
This, you think, though empty-headed –
slowly racing home, a silent extra in a fable

with ants. The sunset on the plain swims
in your short-sightedness; International
Transport threatens to crush you;

a blind hierarchy rules. Where is the house
on the hill with her portrait in the window?
Will you – when all the sheep have gone to sleep –

uncork the night and light a candle; and she,
will she present her husband (hooked on kitsch)
with a dish full of ripe and juicy fruit?

Onward stutters the evening, onward
creeps humanity's procession.
Your happiness throbs like a bloody diesel.

At the Reception

Kissing women through keyholes, wringing
sentiment out of a person or two, drinking
loudmouth-water with nobody – receptions.

Not to mention the plates that go floating
past, crabs that grab you, scowling caviar,
champagne spinning on stems. Birthdays, dinners:

the party-goers are privy to your bank account,
they've caught your wife out in her bottle,
not read your books. But long live Anthropology,

who snarled and tossed a scrap to the hunchback,
sat down on the first field, came up with knives
and forks and set the table with the minor ethics

of manners – on a par with burials or marking
certain days. And so, you blow a glass
to raise, and so, you write a speech

you don't give, sentences screaming
as they plunge into the abyss. There you stand:
staring into your wine. Those present clear your throat,

the throat of the poet, who can't raise his glass
fast enough. Before the cave a wind gets up
to frolic through the chambers of your heart.

Writing Home

The wind sows seagulls over the cold sea;
the gloomy waiter copulates in the kitchen;
a medieval hand scoops mussel shells

from his plate to scrape an arse clean —
but the azure drains from the eyes of the poet
who is thinking of his wife, missing her tongue

at the table: 'Dip the sun in your water glass,
arrange the mountains in your window, then draw
your lover into your southern bed, my dear.'

He splits his nib and scratches out the words
he wants to keep to himself: 'You've stayed so blonde,
my love; the little foxes in the vineyard,

my love; your deer and pomegranates,
my love — what on earth is that incessant
groaning, what are those gulls doing

on my sea of ink?' He washes his shells
and pays the bill; carries her upstairs and sees,
rising in the cynical mirror, the indestructible

temple of her white body. Clambering over
the rocky shore of her wine-coloured sea,
he pushes on, ever closer to her.

A Telephone Conversation With a Friend Who Has Cancer

In memory of Kamiel Vanhole

With chemistry coming out of his pores,
there's only fifty-five kilos of friend left,
coughing up something on the book he's reading –

plus the almost negligible weight of his soul
(located in the pineal gland according
to Descartes). The phone holds its breath,

you, versifier, grip that bone tight like a dog.
His body has grown so thin from the smoke;
the nurses – oh, the hard charity of their hands –

are mission sisters in a colony of the Catholic
king Cancer; the attending physician
is the district head: they murder with kindness,

drip by drip, the smiling bitches, the polite bastard.
Man? Darkness that has caught fire.
Man? A to-do between two silences.

Death is an awkward solution for the riddle of time.
Death is a cack-handed remedy. Just rave on
(you live your life sitting on the ox you seek, says Zen)

until the hospital, hum postmodernism's
incoherent swansong and when it gets
too much, just call the vet.

Old Friend

For Marjan Janssen

The wolves have lain down at your feet,
your kids have started thinking of kids;
acceptance descends on you like gentle rain.

It's how it goes. But your features
are still just as fine, your hair (blonde
with electricity) still curtains your shyness

like the day we met; you have remained
the middle-aged girl you've always been.
We see you in a glass case in Greece:

clay, Attic, budding breasts a couple
of millennia ago – tomorrow a surly farm boy
will plough and sow, but never stroke your toes.

We see you on a dolphin in Pompeii:
the smithy in the mountain must be closed.
We've seen you everywhere since then. Pregnancy

has stretched your belly, you've endured the terrors
of drugs, survived the dirty trick of being
mortgaged; your eyes read this through glasses.

The hellhound snuffles round come sunset.
Turn back the covers! Moisten the earthenware
of your lips. Clasp the glistening fish, Marjan.

Agnostic Evensong

Saint Davids, Wales

In a valley full of psalms and nightingales,
he lay beside a river on the bank of a cathedral
reading the cotton-thread clouds on a violet evening.

Flowering valerian everywhere. Bible-blithe people
bowed their heads like blades of grass and the bells
chimed his personal invitation – it was a *huis clos*

of grace and as the wind erased the writing
of those clouds, he lay there by that water and was
oh so joyous. Death was there as well: a murder

of crows celebrated their vespers of objection,
while the heron-like priest regurgitated a formidable
centuries-old sentence, that every man is a piece

of the Continent etc. Then the choir filled the dish
that seemed to serve him up: the dragonflies
hung in the air, as if planning to settle him...

Calm down, molecules! You're a clod of Europe,
let me embrace you before you wash away and drown,
he thought, confused. But dozed off on valerian.

He lay in that valley listening to the canon for choir
and crows, the holy words, the diaphanous hovering;
and from the bells above him time rained down.

Ars Poetica for a Blonde

It's just a casually hummed thought,
your feigned nonchalance explains. Or else
a clumsy attempt at a dream. Or else

the expression of a rather masculine
longing for a coherent escape
from rationality. And the poet is lying.

Dishing up deceitful dollops of gibberish
for the purpose of penetrating women. To that end
he strews allusions, exhibits his existential

agony, downplays his art with artifice and wit.
And for the rest (pausing briefly for the comma
of your wink) his poem is the phony confession

of a tall dwarf: the criminological profile of a soul
in extremis... Blonde with admiration she stares at you.
And your burning eyes see the incomprehensible love

of this cutie – a hundred thousand years ago
under the stellar ejaculate, around the night-time fire,
you already knew the way to a woman's heart

was through her ear; and now you sing to her eager flesh
that you are made of words and fiery water, you satyr,
who'll sleep it off tomorrow in the old vineyard.

Summer Days

It's a strange kind of summer, with thunder
but no storms, with sudden frequent downpours
in the blazing sun, as if invented by

a mythomane who passionately longs
for miracles that go beyond the scope
of ordinary weather forecasts, things like

a most unusual wind that skims the sea,
which is obedient and crystalline,
while we head for the horizon, my wife and I.

It is a strange kind of summer, suggesting
a soul that floats through the trees and the night,
owl-like, half voracity and half lament

for the pre-conditions of existence:
that the sons of men, made of chemistry
and memories, must finally be lost

in the gathering twilight – unexpected,
quick, silhouetted against a giant moon
for less than a beat, mouseward bound:

a shrill squeak of protein, skin and fur, bones
and all – prey. Charles! Is our malevolence
innocence? But proof is tiresome to truth.

It is a strange kind of summer, with romantic
representations of happiness: the sun
tousles your hair, the rain is warm on your skin,

and by the light of the lightning I write
a love poem for my wife: 'Darling,
the summer is short and almost gone, come,

kiss me, please...' And during this stammering, she unbuttons her blouse and plunges me into the concentric abyss of excruciating bliss.

Father Dreams

I dream of an ancient beckoning mole,
but my hope of a snug hole, with father
and mother mole inviting guests

in to a cosy fire is infantile – instead
I find an underworld of running
and tunnelling, a thousand times a thousand

gleaming black, velvet-hard moles:
powerless I lie on my back
beneath the weight of my revulsion

staring at worms and wood lice; soil
and filth fill my mouth; irrefutable
Darwinism and nothing else.

That is my first dream. Feeble daylight wakes me.
The fridge is starving, the fireplace frozen.
Why I'm here is still unclear.

I eat and drink. I palpate my ego
and my diary hurts. And again
night falls and I dream like a lunatic.

I dream of my father who is dead and lying
between the roots of a linden with his face
grounded in language; vague echoes

of tense melodies: Romanticism menacing
like a thunderstorm, the Rhine rises, an epoch
longs for something great and gets Schubert,

Novalis, Neuschwannstein, suicide and syphilis –
and all of them 200 years under the sod
under exhausted mortals and bare lindens.

That is my second dream. I wake up in an ice-cold
room and it's as if the wind is blasting wisps of grey
around my skull. Black issues from my mouth.

'You're clever at the written word, but not immune
to a better class of sentiment. In end effect,
more mannered than manly, you're somewhat spineless,

wouldn't you say? Don't take it to heart:
you weren't your maker…' That's how the day
frets inside of me. And for the third time the night herds

its sheep, a flock of images waiting
under my window; they look up quizzically,
bleating for attention. And in the first drops of rain

I dream that a buried word of my father's
drills through the earth, a word from a poem
many people love. And he smiles

in the distance at my post-modern vicissitudes,
my vanity, my neuroses. 'Son,' I dream
him saying, 'look after your children like I

looked after you. Worship your wife with your heart
and your cock. Remember me, pour out your words
and don't forget to erase your previous poem.'

The Castaway

In memoriam Eusebio G. (1930-1994)

Imagine:
there is a sailor and his ship goes down.
He swims and makes the coast, the rugged coast,
and now he needs to climb, but weighed down so!
His skin and muscles stinging from the salt,
he feels a breathless giddy longing for
the water down below, the mighty water
where he can rest, the water that will carry him...

I. A Landlocked Wedding

Adrift upon the waters of a Saturday,
how old was I? Was I a knight on horseback
galloping over a field of brown and yellow squares
in a gripping game of chess? Did the world
obey the rules I knew? Or did ten hearts go floating
down the drain when Madame Sosostris let a card
she'd kept for me since 1922
slip through her jewel-encrusted fingers?
'Forget about your horoscope.
What kind of god would scuff his shoe
to write HOPE in the gravel of the stars?
Better off buying the hand of a whore,
who'll love you with the weight of all the West.'

Suddenly the water was ice up to my chest –
in the cellar a fuse blew silently.

And it all came back to me: a man receives nothing,
except it be given him from heaven.
The truth was a blonde woman, a round stone,
a girl almost, from modern Brussels.
The truth was that I, male, forty, wet,
had opened up my heart to her, my clever heart;
it bled in my breast like a pound of beef.
I saw all this in darkness
and in that darkness dried myself.

I counted the days, yet a little while.
I sang of death on my writing pad
and buried my pen in my flesh like a skewer.
I wanted to kill myself, but who was that?

O poetry! Time set to music!

Older, I write the book of someone else.

★★★

My friends got married in offices and chapels.
In Breendonk, it was an orchard full of burning apples:
the sun was just departing as the bride of death
and the province had almost perfected its hush,
when the disco started bashing the night.
A man arrived who was a stranger to my eyes.
Encumbered with the head of an antique king,
lumbered with a peaceful thirst for blood.

'García...! Hola hombre...! Sailor from the Canaries!'

It was buzzing with people swaying away,
poppies in the slumbering depths of the night,
the European night. Never knew there were so many.

The West dissolved in my whisky glass.
I danced slow to a tune I didn't know.
I didn't know my wife, who was doing a tango.

He tasted wine in all the tongues of the world.
He spoke the broken Latin of the ports.
He understood the Hebrew of the heart
and praised in salty Flemish the tool
hung under the sweet abundance of his gut.
And what about you, García? Ever get married?

'Deep in my wine I find truth and Tenerife.'

All things told he was forty-six to sixty-four years old.
He lived on the Left Bank and spent his days playing chess
         with a computer.

In the evenings his room was blue with television.
Shirt undone, he'd smoke Ducados down to his navel, and at night
he'd sometimes write a letter to a woman, his mother.
In the shadow of that other Antwerp lay his island.
He'd often stare upstream, waiting for the tower block to fall.

★★★

The hands to feed us were Frans and Rita's, their fish-
and-chip stand shining in the Scheldt. On the promenade
we puffed for mercy, repentant fire-eaters.

'See the gulls above that Russian tub? They flirt with every boat,
like whores they take the sailors' lonely bread .'
The wind was lazy, the wind had been on his island that day.

We wandered round and round, peripatetic pedestrians,
antique alter egos, uncircumcised by divinity.
The day flew by, the blushing sun returned to her husband.
The old darkness of the poets started stinking like a rose...

'Give us a drink, mademoiselle.'
The woman wrote us down on her hand to remember,
the rocking woman carried us round against her bosom,
carried our heads on a platter.
                       But caresses
in some language or other, the language she happened to speak,
what did they mean? That the charms
of her twenty rhyming arms
could warm this twentieth-century man?
                                 Ash
was my love, ash was the love I longed for.
Night made a mess of his undertaker's suit
(a joke, because he was an artist
installing death and pornography
in the bedrooms of the bourgeoisie).
Was a man ever more than a cigar hanging

from the lips of time? Time had swallowed every tongue,
time had chewed up and spat out every tongue,
time spoke in tongues through me, through me,
in whom heaven burnt like hell.
                                    'Long live
the metropolis, long live the metropolis, long live...
but first another drink, mademoiselle.'

Later it was Saturday and I got home.
My key was broken and took its time
to fit just as I took time to see
this lock not fitting the key in my hand.
My morning paper was sticking out of the slot next door.
Standing by the Museum of Fine Arts,
a painter and a poet, together
under the chestnuts, overlooking an expanding
big bang of balls: the better-off Bohemians
were playing pétanque. We waved hello. Like a thief
in the day I opened my address. In a calm, deep
bed in gentrified South Antwerp I would sink away and sleep,
sink away but wake me. Yet a little while.

'What you get married for if you don't want children?'

II. Ashkenazic

You're good company in this Belgian town,
now the night is as tepid as the Coke in the glass
of the girl who wants to sing karaoke,
but doesn't have a song to call her own.
'Don't you feel like it, honey?'
The neon *Sud* writes our south
in the eyes of passing women.
Businessmen in restaurants suck the souls out of six oysters.
And through all this, May mixes sweet lilac,
flowering in a backyard near the synagogue.

I call this place by its pagan dactyl, *Antwerpen*.
I get by in my vernacular and dream
of a room with a view of all the streets of Europe.
I'm not sure which neurosis I should sanctify,
now that I've settled here until the coming dawn.

We sit here in Belgium explaining our lives.
We sit out the night at an outdoor cafe
where a girl wants to sing karaoke,
but waits for the boy who's more than a friend.
'Watch one hour with me...'
When she plucks the soft lies from his lips
the bubbles go to her head.
How far will the water carry her voice?

The Left Bank despondency comes walking over the water.
Don't think of your room, your table, anything else in Brabosch.
Don't think of the black bird, the Ashkenazic spirit
that spreads its wings, screeches, batters your window.
Here, there, on the square of this Christian cathedral,
on your island – for fifty years you've been foreign everywhere.
Drink this life, drink it, or slurp the soul from a living oyster.

Near *Shomre Hadass* I live in a bourgeois home
in Judaism's obstinate shadow.
I keep a clean room for you there
and turn a soft stone for your pillow.

— I wrote this because I was scared you were lonely.

III. Men

The evening star sidles over to the moon above the river.
I face him in this enigmatic restaurant
and tell a dead man's tales,
hoping for an aperitif
that will open my mouth and confess my unhappiness.
Every word is a word at our throats.
And emerging from the river in the window is a blonde
whose red hair is turning black as night
and my head drifts along in my thoughts to the sea –
but the smiling waitress coming to serve us
looks like a transvestite.

And you, García, what do you have to say?

'Let's drink to your sorrow.
You were so keen to love with a passionate intellect
and think to the clink of inexplicable verse.
You're the straw that sucks June dry to the cherry,
the way the night outside drinks up the river.'

Our sorrow never wears the same dress twice.
So together we took the train from Brussels
to a room with all-encompassing walls
and a greedy Paris hotel bed
where she brought death to his knees with her bare hands.
Anyway. The rest is one big anyway.
This fucking wine is full of cork.

And what about you, García? Go on, talk.
You stir the ash and laugh about my flirting, my hurting.

'The girl whose hair brought you to grief
has cut your heart like so much beef.'

The ashtray smokes like a crack in the ground, my glass falls.
My head, my hard head, rests on twisted limbs.
Then slowly, slowly, I wake to the first squalls
across the water, on the quay, against the guttering restaurant:
the woman with the bill is already the ghost of a man.
We are here in this Western harbour, this Antwerp,
far from some unknown perfecting divinity.

Outside you smell my sadness as a whisky OD.
You throw the first words into the water
and when the wind blows through you on the corner
you sing a song about happy days in Brussels.

And you, what about you?

'I've done what I can do.'

IV. Thoughts

It's not the times in the paper that are terrible
or the fate of our apocalyptic alter egos
or the history of the year 5760
in Antwerp. Please do not read poetry
but look deep into your TV screen
because time itself is terrible. Try
to look me in the eye, see a face appear.
Look into the warm red of the wine and see red.
How, my wife, should your eyes be opened?
No god spits upon earth to smear
mascara on your lashes... And now you're not listening,
kill time and seize your days! Yes, time must die:
his face is abhorrent to us and few
can bear to look on it. Only neurotics
dare to stare, we, the damned chosen, we keep
our gaze on that face. I could describe it,
I could describe it, I could describe it
as that blizzard in the Ardennes when
night shot his stormful of arrows straight at our car —
but that would lack an edge and be, well, poetry.
      Maybe
once this mortal, the monarch who was the son
of a monarch, gave a human face to blind time,
to the terrible category from Königsberg. You,
fortunately, are not mad, not European enough
to see a king in a Christian name. You saw
King Albert tremble and were moved yourself.

As a child, I played a lot of chess with my father.

Someone once said that no-one could be alone with himself.
Whoever said so was like a shepherd of thought:
this very night I sat bleating in a bar about a woman
trying to forget I had to die this very night. The night

came down, the night destroyed the bourgeoisie and I
myself was the bourgeoisie. I write this to hold my peace with you,

yet someone must speak in a loud voice,
of all of us, one of us must speak quote unquote
and sing for the girl in the karaoke bar
who wants to wake the drunken youth because she loves him so.
And it has to be about something, not about nothing.

By learning to play chess, I learnt how to lose.

V.   Friends

The cathedral arose on a holiday slide:
his picture window overflowed
with pink champagne the sky had broken out
to toast the world, the dining city,
the slow bend in the Scheldt, the fish restaurants
on the *plage* of Sint-Anneke (the smell of searing oil
drifting over the water) and García's high-rise,
which was never as beautiful as here. The view
made my head spin on his balcony, for a second
it was like sleepwalking or anaesthetic:
in one ungodly moment everything fell and fell until
I kissed his cheeks on entering.
He was cooking through reading glasses,
frying up savoury dreams of Spain
in clouds of tobacco smoke and browsing
in a letter from his mother, some thirty years dead.
'She never even got to stick a smiling king on the envelope
and still I have this top-heavy infantile longing
to return to someone or something
spinning round inside my head
(Tenerife...! Tenerife...!)
until I fall asleep.'
We stilled our hypocritical hunger and drank
with him to the bride from Breendonk and a groom
who had sailed under the flag of the Canaries –
and through the sky danced the indigo evening gown
of a girl with gel in her hair.

His wooden computer was counting on a king's side castle.   47

Further, further south a Ferris wheel scooped up
men and women stuffed with chips, fear and fertility.
the fair had laid anchor on its annual quay
and Antwerp thrilled to a schmaltzy pulse.

In the ghost house an inconsolable ghost
was shaking, shaking on his squeaking spring.
A fan of playing cards under ten
resolute fingertips, ten tapping red nails,
told Cheryl that her teddy bear in shining armour
was on his way to carry off her virginity
(nothing much new since 1922).

                And this opposite bank
was a dazzling reflection: I (or someone) realised
that the fair cut vain, vain Antwerp
the way a Jew cuts a diamond.

                And I, a man of forty, rode
my flying horse and looked down on the world
without love – I acted like a child
and stuck out my tongue.

                But in the clear mist of years
that filled him, García greeted on his island
the nameless merry-go-round donkey: with firm hand
his father led him round in the inexplicable
mystery of anchored giddiness, the drunken
clarity which is also poetry...

One by one the fairground lights turned off the South.
Rain and wind harried the scenery.
We have to escape from this tower,
mimed the American woman's mouth –
we need to break free of this hour
and the walls closing in on me.

The Left Bank melancholy walked over the water,
the moon's soliloquy drifted out to sharks at sea,
the passing Arab hawked and spat,
the rain swelled and washed our four feet lovelessly.

In the car I didn't say a word, although I longed to speak.

    ★★★

'We're no family, no six litres of cloying lemonade apiece.
We don't give ourselves to each other as lovers
so that Western romanticism can turn us into lighter,
better people for a couple of years if we're lucky.
We don't see each other as a man with a knife
in search of foreskins, or a half-grown girl in tights,
or the unreliable blue of a postman
emerging from the haze of early morning
with a posthumous letter in his hand.
                                        No, we
are friends, friends. With a duty
to celebrate birthdays. A duty to speak
to kill the silence, to silence the chill
that has already crept under our clothes,
under our skin.
                        I tell you:
friends, I say, this is my task, our task.
Please take me at my word. Reply. But
you don't answer, you don't speak but keep
your distance, and your silence comes no closer.
And I turn my face away. Because there is no father,
no traitor, there is no one. Just the garbage chute
of the loner next door who has to make do
and do it by himself. Rain hits the roof
of all my homes, and the silence is stilled.

The brief romance of your lilac is over.'

VI. Death of a King

What happened then? Was it night and the distant lightning
of a TV image that struck me, or was it morning
and did the phone ring? Either way,
the news came in the raucous Latin of everyday,
and I couldn't ignore it. Printer's ink flowed
from the mouths of heads of state, but heads of state
fell to earth. And also the erudite lackeys
of obscurantism with their desiccated brains –
they too fell to earth. And rock stars,
who sang the times with heavier hand than we,
the poets (though our lies were more honest) – they too
fell to earth. There were but few whose death
was not absurd and somehow unforgettable.

'The less tangible the palm, the more memorable.'

I don't remember how I knew. I only know
I tried to stay up and write: I charged my pen and wrote into the night,
as angry at her as at the unspeakable. I searched
for a word so furious it would cut off an ear,
and didn't find it, and pressed my nib so hard it split.

No. I knew it
the way I know the things I do not know
that are written all the same in my dry hand.
Listen to me, this happened:
a light was burning in the black square of my window.
I felt empty and full of myself and as strange
as a hunger artist. And my heart hoped to speak a Hebrew
that was understood by all, but made do with translations.
            Voilà,
then the day dawned, my front door choked on the newspaper,
someone shouted something in their best Antwerp Dutch...
And my writing pad said:

'The leaves of the palm overshadow our reason.'
A summa? A truth? (A riddle? Fear of something big.)

I threw away my heart and laid my head down on a stone.

★★★

On the day in question, someone emerged
from the lift like a stowaway,
to visit in the hours that followed Cloud Nine,
like a deaf-and-dumb nostalgic nobody
constantly seeing faces of vague acquaintance
in the red twilight of the Skippers' Quarter...
Was it like that? (This is a reconstruction, so I may
be wrong.) Summer and winter the electric tongues
flicker in the fireplace like a burning
bush of pleasure; summer and winter
indeciduous hits burst without warning
from the jukebox like strippers from a cake;
summer and winter, the girls milk the myth,
sipping fizz with precious gestures, they pay
no mind to the discrete transvestite
softly scratching his thighs (the itch goes right
up under his suspender belt). A clammy heat
hung now, August, above the bar. The clock melted.
It was time for sluggish initiative: finally
García began speaking above his Stella ashtray
to Ann, or Sabina, or Dominique, or Ann –
not many women's names that suit a man.
'He was sweating like a pig in his shirtsleeves!
The shadow of the ceiling fan slid
over his unbuttoned chest hair. Like
a big grey knife that kept slashing at him,
I thought... And then he fell over, his head
rolled into my lap, as if he were in a hurry,
and yet so slow, so slow,

as if that blink of an eye took a thousand years.
And Johnny dialled emergency
and I just didn't know what to do,
so all I did, the whole time was say,
"hombre, no, hombre, no, hombre..."
but I don't know if he heard me.'

– García! You heard it, didn't you? You heard the siren sing
        her ancient song?

They rushed him to the Saint Elisabeth under the malevolent blue
of a flashing light, and a woman's stone-cold-sober scream flew
around the corner, but the man she desired
was a strapped-down hero. His mask was breathing hard.
He disappeared into a building.

                        And we, the poor living,
sat by a white bed and saw impatient time
chewing on a cigar.

                        Further down the road,
a gathering of the theatre-loving bourgeoisie
in Cleopatra's palace:
strands of smoke still drifting under the dome,
the summer fashion rustled, the snake skins had been shed
seductively in the cloakroom. Now she was sitting pretty,
her sweet face smoothed into attentive self-pity,
like a rescued draft. All this love made her uneasy,
as difficult as the unrelenting metre and this queen's impossible bed.
'You bring the cure of all our ills... The adder.'
Necklace beads clicked. The absolute other,
the stone in the grass, the fast shadow, the cold genius
biting into her life... Silence. The simple scale
of an ambulance ripped the poetry.

The polyglot who appeared at the foot of his bed
had mould on his chin and round lenses

that showed me pre-war Europe.
'Master,' I said. 'Is there hope?'
His tight smile made sixty-four years
fly by on his ice-cold pocket watch.
He mumbled underneath his breath in French:
'L'homme n'est qu'un cigare à la bouche du temps.'

He disconnected the oxygen hose.
He pulled on his trench coat.
He put on his felt hat and disappeared.

I said something in broken Spanish
and my distraught, indecent words
were taut with truth, they betrayed me.

She, in my tears, slowly let go of his hand.

VII. December

'Write on the ground!' A male voice spoke,
and my thoughts were like driftwood,
floating over the water to some Brazilian shore,
where he listened, the happy castaway,
to serrated shells with a calyx of pink,
and the ocean bore coral reefs, languages, simple
Phoenician ships. In a fabric of quotations
I wrapped him (it smelt of cloves),
lines of verse washed up. 'As the manner
of the Jews is to bury...' But the rain
lay its small hands on the South, and my face evaporated
in the magnifying mirror. And we began to speak
of necessity, man and woman on this slow
silver film of a day. 'No cemetery in Antwerp
is going to have him. No crows will swarm
around him. No rainwater will collect
in the hard data on his stone.'

(Repatriation by the kilo. Her month's salary.
In our deaf telephone, 'Never been there, Tenerife.
Toughest steaks in the world, apparently.')

You, who wandered the sea's blue rooms,
and could colour the ocean with a drop of wine,
and heard the rocks singing while bound to the mast,
who gave me the key to your shore: I strapped
your ticking watch onto my wrist, collected paraphernalia,
closed the door forever. And what about you, García,
            with my dry eyes,
the image of Clark Gable in your seaman's book –

It is deep in December now that I'm writing this for us
in the sprung rhythm of the last days. And I, I
who have to forget a man I didn't know and move the insides

of clocks, women, shells, stones, intellectuals
and of America that's pounding in my empty head,
now have to, in this night of yet a little while,
now have to raise my eyes to your blue eyes,
because somebody has to do it and I am somebody,
to do it now while I still can, now,

and yet a little while.

Notes to 'The Castaway':

During World War II, Breendonk was the site of an infamous German concentration camp.

Brabosch is a Jewish name for Antwerp. *Shomre Hadass*, the 'Guardians of the Faith', is the main synagogue of the Ashkenazic Jews, close to the Scheldt in South Antwerp.

Königsberg was home to Immanuel Kant, the first to define time and space as philosophical categories.

A Public Woman

A verse play in three acts

'I grow old... I grow old...'
T.S. Eliot

'...*ce visage a eu lieu.*'
Marguerite Duras

The only character is COCO, a sixty-year-old actress.
The piece is set in the theatre in which it is performed.
The time is 'neither night-time nor day', 1996.

I

How old am I? I'd rather save that question
for later in the evening. Much more pressing:
how old are we, all of us, humanity?
Before we wrote, there was no humanity.
Before we read, there was no humanity.
Humans existed, but that's a different story.
A boy squatted between two mighty rivers –
the muddy god Euphrates and his brother:
a nodding day, the hot and thirsty cattle
drank at the flowing breast of one of the gods,
they chewed their cud and bent to drink some more.
Languid silence, buzzing insects. The boy
appraised his surroundings. Time was always, absolute –
it stifled him. He took a broken branch
and started poking at the dark wet clay:
his formless doodles grew the horns of cattle.
The water mumbled, the sky above grew bright
and vast, with so much time still left to kill.
Lonely, he drew a hut to house his homesick self...
And so: when I write A, I tame a bull.
And so: when I write B, I build a house.
For seven thousand years, we have been writing
history, and we remain undaunted by
the absolute indifference of Time –
that 'we' is Mesopotamians and Greeks,
and humanists and Romantics and us
as well. We make a lengthy story! But:
'We do not know very much of the future
Except that from generation to generation
The same things happen and again.
Men learn little from others' experience.
But in the life of one man, never
The same time returns.' Unquote. It's from
a book gone missing in my head. Meaning?

Humanity, poor humanity:
in seven thousand years of humanity
two generations have arisen. No more.
Not hundreds, only two. Parents and children.
Parents and children. All those fucking parents
and all their fucking children: we just keep
appearing and disappearing in that form,
as if a giant Ferris wheel scoops up
the fear of death that haunts our sideshow alleys,
raises our passions to high heaven, then
dumps life back down upon the earth, etc.
That wheel is Time and turning, turning, turning.
My father took me now and then. I must
have been quite small and even he was scared.
We held each other tight like enemies.
Parents and children. The natural first theme.
I'm talking Hamlet and Electra here.
I'm talking Oedipus and me.

                    And me?
As far as I'm concerned: I'm an actress,
a presence on the stage since time began.
I have been every woman known to man:
the girlish mistress, the scheming intriguante,
naivety herself with phoney curls...
Let's say I know a thing or two about
the mechanics of masculine desire.
(Theme number two, the sweet civil war
between the sexes: I'll get back to that
a little later on.) Let's not forget:
I made a quite divine dead Juliet.
Subsequently I ripened into roles
in which eroticism stuttered. Examples:
the housebound spouse, the hysteric, the queen.
My children's murderess, a loving wife
to my own son...I've been all of these
and there were times it made me feel (my mind

descending to my breasts, my gut, my legs)
just like a Viennese quack's finger puppet.
Time has taken its impassive knife
to my face. An unforgiving signature,
thank God no audience can make it out,
so they tell me... What did my teacher say?
'The word *character,* children, means engraved.'
That's what she said... My Greek teacher... My God,
what am I doing blathering on like this?
My bloody nerves are playing up. But why?
My tongue twists into knots. I am a woman
about to make her debut in the theatre
of old age – that's something I never wanted!
This, I'm afraid to say, is my third theme.
Where is my jeune premier? I'm all alone.
I've never stood here this alone before.
People consider me a public woman:
that's neither here nor there, it comes with the job –
I'm seen, therefore I am. I'm not ashamed
to admit it. I am an artistic coquette,
such an artistic demimondaine... Immune
to words. But surely not an old grey woman
posing on pink cushions before grey men,
disappointment from head to foot? Look at me!
As blonde as blonde and still I feel so grey.
I just don't get it. They stare at me
and I'm afraid. With death in every eye,
every I must die: it's even got me rhyming.
I'll just turn off the light...

                            And now it's dark.
Where are my thoughts? At war. It's World War II
and I've forgotten to remember that it's war.
How old am I? I've just been put to bed
by Lieve, who rents out her hard red hands
to Mama dear – my mother is all dresses,
anaemic smiles and spells of feeling faint.
How could she possibly play mummy too,

let alone attend to washing up or cut
recalcitrant potatoes down to size?
It was the maid who heard me say my prayers,
turned off the light without a kiss and said:
'Sleep tight, Coco,' (Coco's my name, you see)
and packed darling little Coco away
in the velvet chocolate box of the night.
I cuddle close to my stuffed animals,
my leaking threadbare bear, my hairy monkey:
alone in my child's bed I must make do
with these companions. Half asleep I say:
'Lieve's a thief cause she's stolen a ring...'
I told my mother that first thing this morning,
she'll let her go before the day is out.
I've taken my revenge on the wrong woman.
(Despite my never seeing her again,
she still appears accusingly in dreams:
'You stole that ring yourself, didn't you, Coco?'
she says. 'Where is it now?' She fades away.)
This is my first intrigue. I search for love,
but no one ever hugs my seven years:
my mother is an ice-cold empress who
rejects her; spineless Papa holds his tongue
or mumbles through his granite newspaper;
I get a goodnight cross on my forehead.
A court that Shakespeare would have liked, no wonder
I enlist my Mr Bear and Mr Monkey
in childish conspiracies, I love myself,
and dig for hidden secrets...
                              I wake up.
And see my fear dissolve in the light of day
like Alka Seltzer in a glass of water –
leaving only concentration. Thank God.
The war is over. Not inside of me,
as yet, but peace is boring for a child.
What's more, much smaller fears are now afoot.
I go to school, I come back home. My mother's

paying a visit to the priest; the maid
(this latest Lieve's name has slipped my mind)
hardly looks up across the kitchen table,
too busy polishing silver against the clock.
It's just gone four. The house is mine alone.
The silence is so tense the creaking hurts
as I sneak up the stairs. The landing's swathed
in ambiguous shadows, hush: *Papa?!*
So still, my heart skips a beat.
Ridiculous – pomaded Papa's safe
behind his desk at the Commercial Bank.
My hand gropes in the vase and grabs the key:
my parents' door is smirking horribly
as I deliberately unlock their room.
Twin beds beneath a single counterpane.
A folding floral screen. How motionless
all these things are! It's been an endless week
and nothing here has changed. *So look at me,*
commands the dressing table mirror, *Look –*
I can still see that waxen, haughty child,
no beauty, but resolved she will become one.
I don't have any friends, I have myself.
I play alone. Messrs. Monkey and Bear
now pine away, away in a corner,
their place usurped by Gus, my ginger tom:
alive, he purrs, he licks, he sleeps in my bed.
Oh God. Oh Gus. Out of the blue, burning
curiosity has now infected Coco.
A tongue. A fingertip. *Look at yourself!*
The book is on my mother's bedside table:
we all read books to see if we appear

within their pages; and I have now been here
two Wednesdays running, reading in a fever –
as much as my inadequate brain allows
in French – this book which scalds my hands. '*Jeune filles…*'
Oh God. My God. Today I meet myself.
Reeling through seven thousand years and one

second, I make the door, the hall. Escape.
Fleeing into my bedroom, running from life
to life. I drive out Gus the ginger tom.
Downstairs! Ravenous beast! I pray. I feel.
That open wound of mine! My clammy skin.
Miaow ten Hail Mary's.
                              Pure from fright,
I stay pathetically devout for three long years.
The third of which is set in boarding school,
a convent school where sombre nuns spend days
on end correcting Mama's French in me –
a drab French-speaking town provides the backdrop.
I can still smell the beeswax in the hall,
a smell that gets into my clothes. And still
I sometimes see my class arise and feel
Ma Mère's exacting gaze (as grey as iron)
go scraping once again down our brown dresses;
even now I hear the whispering of the dorm,
and all the giggles. *I* just lie there listening,
without a friend. I never get homesick,
except for God knows what. And God is what
I've got. I'll serve Him as a mission nun...
The night turns off my thoughts.
                              My confirmation
is coming closer, my first solemn communion.
In spring, that year in spring. I kneel in chapel:
the bishop lays his hands upon my head,
and now the finger with the blessèd ring
is rubbing chrisom on my clammy forehead.
I feel excitement. Incense spirals up.
A penetrating smell that overcomes
the thirteen years inside my wedding dress:
I am a mystic making love with God
(how strange that my as yet unnamed narcissism
is broad enough for a divinity).
The chic two-piece in the distance is my mother,
observing from behind a white-washed pillar

while I stand blushing like a pallid rose...
Plenty of women went through something similar,
I'm told. A religious phase, the first awareness
that time will not stand still, a niggling fear
of imminent adulthood, that kind of thing.
But what came next was mine alone. What came
was stomach-ache, that very afternoon.
Cramps. And then blood, red blood. Awaited now
for three long years, it's finally come and made
a stain on that white wedding dress of mine,
a stain that's kept on growing to this day –
I hardly hear the smothered gasps and giggles,
I only hear my mother's voice, saying,
'*Ah, mon enfant! Mes félicitations!*
T'es une jeune fille maintenant...' She disappears
again in that red haze. I am surprised
that I'm not really shocked. I'm a woman,
I think. It's not too bad. A little woozy.
Where's God got to? I've read *Le mariage*
parfait. About the ebb and flood. About
my blood and how it has to boil over.
The moon sucks at my soul... Where is my mother?
I open up my eyes. And look. She's wandering
into a gloomy gallery with *Ma Mère*.
In her two-piece. Pink hat.

                             From this point on,
nothing is quite the same. I get lovesick
for the love I never get. At my bedside
a doctor with a pince-nez lisps in Latin
about iron in my blood. Don't make me laugh!
The Traction Avant is there to pick me up,

Papa behind the wheel: final handshake
with dear *Ma Mère*, the engine roars its laughter
through the gates and sends the gravel flying
round her ears. The catechism slams shut
behind my back. *Adieu*, women in black.
But this small man who's rabbiting away,

nose up against the windscreen (collecting stamps
is my poor father's one abiding passion),
is just as strange. I'm now an apostate
from my own parents... Approaching Brussels the sun
avidly licks my face.
                              A brand new school
in walking distance from our house. And there
I stand, between two hundred blue-clad strangers,
lost in a courtyard, my Walloon pinafore
browner than ever. I'm seen until it hurts.
And heard, my rusty Flemish... (Exercise:
give synonyms. Coco at the blackboard.
'Three words or euphemisms for *to die.*'
With ridiculously squeaking chalk I write
decease. The class is staring at my back.
I think. I sweat. My mind's a blank. I have
no mother tongue.) And I'm not even pretty,
not yet. As thin as a reed, a reed that broods,
the chill wind blows its tunes right through me as
I cycle through the provincial hinterland
of the dead town my parents call home –
blonde with desire, a *garçonne* who hangs out
with boys' school boys, smokes cigarettes and watches
blue flowers float up from their lips (they're much
too shy to blow me lies). Meanwhile I dream
immense and hazy dreams about a woman
who'll burst upon the scene like a volcano,
go hidden in wisps of flimsy cloud, and tower
high on those superhuman legs of hers
above defeated men, and speak in a voice
that melts the very stones... That's how I'll be.
I'm suffering from a bad case of '*Le désir*
de paraître', to borrow from Duras...
and all the while I'm as cold as Coca Cola:
without the slightest bit of interest in
the seedy bars that youths frequent, not yet:
I am my only interest. Gus the cat

is allowed to visit me, and play with me,
and I play with myself, vaguely ashamed...
Then comes a day that turns me upside-down.
Sometimes the complicated lives we lead
give way before one incandescent moment:
in the depths of time, something happens. And me,
I see the glorious One Day that is
my destiny: at fifteen my heart blazes
like a fire that's thawed at last. Perhaps I sound
too feminine. It can't be helped. What happened
was a school excursion, to the cinema.
Propitious circumstance (I spend too long
combing my hair in the ladies') guides me to
the wrong theatre, where *Der blaue Engel*
has just begun. I find a seat. Unrath,
that strict, old-fashioned teacher, is entering
the grey and flickering cabaret where Lola
works as a hostess, throwing leg after leg
into the air... That's her! I've found the woman
of my dreams! She's it! She's wearing her top hat,
she's wearing her suspenders! God, give me
one of those legs... I hear an ocean surging
in that deep voice – '*Ich bin von Kopf bis Fuss
auf Liebe eingestellt...*' I drown in plush.
Lola-Lola and Herr Professor Unrath.
Back home he cherishes her photograph,
through reading glasses he investigates
the little downy feathers dolling up
the paper Lola, and his tender breath
caresses those long legs. And I am sure
that I can feel his breath. I'm also sure
(as sure as only the absurd can be)
that it is up to me to instigate
this feverish moment in the barren lives
of thousands... Oh, so blonde is my ambition
as I emerge and move among the girls
in a cloud of knowing: I'm going to become

Marlene Dietrich! (It wasn't till much later
that I got to see her other movies too,
films like *Blonde Venus* and *Shanghai Express*:
within the fatal genealogy
of Garbo, Dietrich, Monroe and Madonna –
all the way back to Sarah Bernhardt who,
in the words of one of her contemporaries,
could not descend a spiral staircase without
the staircase wrapping itself voluptuously
around her, and awash with Garbo's haze
of dreams, and marked forever by the death
of Marilyn Monroe, whose platinum
reflected on the face of JFK,
an afterglow until that fatal day –
in this entire genealogy
of great, impossible women, extending
up to that cold and tinselled soul, Madonna,
Dietrich is still the only one for me.
I often lie in bed and think of her,
I think about my younger years, and think
of Time and how it sank its teeth
into the Lola's flesh I had back then...)

Yes, childhood memories! Parents and school;
that first and archetypal cigarette;
the casually discarded match with which
the cool, inevitable angel calmly
lights up his sword: decisively he points
into the world. A flaming sword. The gate
yawns on its hinges: then closes forever
on our childhood paradise... It's odd,
I mean, adulthood doggedly remembers
the same old stuff... Paradise! A word
you always hear from people who've forgotten
what childhood was really like! But I'm
getting ahead of myself.
                              That very summer

I fall in love for the first time, in love
with someone other than myself. I've spent
so long in preparation! Months on end
I haven't gone to bed without my ritual:
I place a chair before the washbasin,
put on a generous coat of lipstick and
extend my longest leg. I look at me,
I clear my throat... 'Coco's going to Hollywood,'
my husky mirror murmurs through the mouth
that I've just painted on. The wound is red,
the fruit is ripe and splits when I exclaim:
'Oh, kiss me, darling, please!' That's how I wait,
waiting for someone nameless, still. I dream
confused and troubling dreams in which this Someone
sometimes reveals himself with a human face,
but mostly he remains the purest Nobody,
a force, a demon, an overwhelming presence...
And then those empty nights of spring give way
to summer holidays. To my surprise
I get to go and stay with Papa's sister,
who I am crazy about. Aunt Isabel
(a young widow, hardly an aunt at all,
she deems the role despicable: for me,
an only child, she's much more like a sister)
lives with her son of seventeen, Philippe,
in a dilapidated country villa
that she inherited from her late husband.
It has a pond, an empty stable, ivy,
romantic disrepair; the friendly cancer
of weeds is omnipresent... Languid days
of pure delight! 'God's never in a hurry
to read the book of July,' says Isabel.
Through sluggish balmy evenings crane flies dance
out on the terrace while the earth unwinds
and slowly closes its greyish-silver pond,
and we exist and drink sweet wine that never
runs out. And I become as sultry as

the summer night: the restless candles lick
at my red glass, I feel the warmth of his leg
against my own... The sky is almost blue
by the time we rise to make our ways to bed,
our empty glasses set with pearls of dew...
We pass our days with reading and drawn-out walks,
we laze away. But when the tepid evening
arrives, it's time to repeat that mythic moment
of yearning inactivity: a moment
that lasts for hours... Until my last night there.
Earlier than usual, Isabel retires.
(Fortuitous coincidence? Design?
The slightest smile's playing on her lips.)
Immediately, I'm not sure how much later,
it happens to me. A hard relentless god
destroys something. Stupidity itself,
I mutely murmur 'darling' to the man
who's covering the girl I try to be.
My flesh is greedier than me. The room
perspires. His marble turns to milk and I
softly call his name. He's silent, stony.
Despondency I still cannot explain
hovers over our bed.
                        I write. He doesn't.
Another boyfriend. Brussels. And the theatre,
the sacred monsters entering my life...
'How ever did you manage?' (My daughter's question,
because men Marina's age can only
pour forth their soul into a prophylactic,
an empty balloon.) I really just don't know.
Would I have led a different life? What if
Philippe had written back... I've no idea.
I wander like a desert nomad, from here
to there, from stage to stage, from nowhere much
to nowhere else. And most of all, from self
to self to self. My Hollywood. But still,
I'm married to a lovely businessman...

And yet, my house is just magnificent…
Civilisation. My God! I just don't know.
I really don't know who the hell I am.

II

Here, where it is neither night-time nor day, neither evening
          nor dawn,
here, in the truthful illusion, in the illusory truth of theatre,
here, where I call out to everyone in particular that I want love,
and where there is nothing I'd like more than to bury my face
in all those hands from all those plays, but face everyone's gaze
and let all my old hands, Medea's and Lady Macbeth's,
sink slowly with these two hands of mine –
here, a lightning zigzag rips my memory open
          like a tin of soup...
About a year or so ago I saw the dead Dietrich.
It was terrible and magnificent. First of all, her voice!
her voice emerging from a coincidental TV:
I was cloistered in a hotel, zapping my boredom
from my misplaced double bed, up and down the scale,
when suddenly some art channel or other came into my room.
Her voice was unmistakeable, bruised, creaking in American
          German and Berlin English,
but no less her voice for all of that.
Time backfired through more than forty years,
as if the waters were rising up once more to smash themselves
          once more upon the rocks:
it sounded *that* eternal. I know no better word.
If she could hear me, Marlene, she'd crack up laughing,
because her sarcasm (with the nurtured vulgarity
          of a well-brought-up girl)
was devastating: death's laughter echoed in her self-mockery.
For a few minutes my thoughts fluttered like a hypnotised moth
before that gently burning screen. It was a German
          documentary,
riddled with archive footage and bluish snippets from her films.
And all the while, a nosy camera tracked through her
          Parisian apartment,
the tomb where she played out the closing scenes

73

of that undead life.
Oversized rooms. Photos. Baubles. And every tangible memory
made the emptiness worse. I could almost hear
        the swollen words
of dead poets, could almost smell the sour milk of dead lovers...
        Despondency.
And then I consciously saw what I wasn't seeing.
Dietrich! You sex bomb defused by Time's disposal squad!
You no longer dared appear before the eye of the world.
Only your voice was left. Only your voice, creaking like a door:
'*Ich bin von Kopf bis Fuss* ridiculous...' Oh fuck,
        was all I thought.

It made me think back, it makes me think back to Brussels
        in the fifties.
The giddiness with which I stumbled, the province
        breathing down my neck,
straight into my apartment! The Rue N'importe, the depths
        of the inner city
(all thanks to Isabel). Sudden sunlight, a moment's
        disorientation after turning the key
on that very first day... A happiness verging on panic followed.
The template of my adulthood appearing before my eyes:
pre-war furniture, dried-out lino, the low-pressure metronome
ticking away in the sink, the shattered mirror which
        split my head to shards,
dead flowered wallpaper... And so on. A socialist version
        of poverty. In short, a dream.
Here, blonde Coco installed herself like a princess, received
        her courtiers,
who emerged spontaneously after lessons, and was happy.
The word may sound ludicrous coming from me, but I
        was happy all the same.
I flitted from party to party, from bar to bar,
traded one careless love in on the next, and laughed
        the time away;
the froth of pleasure was on my wayward lips.

Like the bubbles in our beer, there was no holding me down.
Freedom. But absolute freedom is bad for artists,
as what's-his-name once said. And so, one way or another,
I worked till late at night, free, free, and simultaneously
imprisoned in a circle of electric light... And I, the blonde,
followed Dietrich's example: I tamed my voice, bringing
          its high song down an octave,
because my image demanded that I sound as if it had been years
since I'd had anything but bourbon for breakfast.
I droned out my lines: speaking the words of unknown selves
to the stubborn rhythm of my kitchen tap. For example:

> ...how *fea*tures *are* a*broad*,
> I am *skill*-less *of*; but, *by* my *modesty*,
> The *jew*el *in* my *dow*er,

                    And so on:
Prospero's daughter in *The Tempest*. I fell asleep still pitching
on those seas of verse and learnt to dream a mother tongue
my mother hadn't taught me. Ah, Mama! Did I torment her
with my acting? *Tant mieux, maman...* And if my ruthless stressing
          had Papa's feeble blessing,
the irrepressible Isabel turned out to be a devotee:
          I was invulnerable.
There was more to it. Besides my voice (marinated now in time
much more than whisky), there was also my body.
'Acting, children, is active. Active. Active!'
Despair. Furious gestures. The clumsy gymnastics of dying.
That reminds me of Dietrich again. An absurd segment
in that programme: she's standing before a firing squad.
No blindfold. Frozen smile. Twelve aching rods of steel.
(1935, or thereabouts: a colossal realism was in fashion
          at the time.
Then too, I thought.) Just before the climax one of the soldiers
          snaps,
archetype of the heroic wimp: refusing to shoot a woman.
What's Dietrich do? She touches up two icy lips...

And then the bullets fly. End quivering snippet.
'*So ein Quatsch!*' was all she had to say.
But taken back to those forgotten pages,
she suddenly remembered asking von Sternberg, Josef,
whose directing credits included *The Blue Angel*,
how she should fall. Forwards? Or backwards?
'How should *I* know? I've never been executed
          in my life before...'
That was it. Move. Take the exaggeration of the fifties,
and exaggerate it a tad. Glamour. A strumpet,
          in my mother's eyes.
Merde! The accusations pelted down on Saturdays.
The hips of a whore. A girl around town. *Look, Mama,*
          I'm beautiful!
(On the other hand. How could you expect
          a Coco to understand
that you were anxious on my behalf, but shut up like a crab
          in the timorous, neurotic shell
of the bourgeoisie? For more than sixty years you had
          a pale longing for something
beyond your perfect marriage, something you couldn't name
          in any language you knew,
until it grew, hard and present, in your flesh. Cancer.
They broke you open. And left you broken and open.
I hear a quiet blubbering when we speak.)

But then the real acting started. The seriousness with which
          I still...
how can I explain? put on another life. Like a ship
          putting into port:
the exhilaration of shore-leave in foreign familiar territory.
In buzzing bars. The languid lingua franca of the seas
in the mouths of tight-lipped men now pouring out their hearts
to some exotic Lola. A crooner crowing love songs.
The heat melts like chocolate. They'll have their little death
in a back room soon enough. Badly needing to be somebody
          yet nobody at the same time,

it's all too human... Am I being unclear? Again.
I put on another life, like a transvestite putting on a dress.
I strut my second skin and hair. I'm someone, no one,
        make-up and repartee,
and when I take this self off and come back to me, I die a little...
Imagine that it's really true and our minds actually make
a furious short of our lives which really does get shown
once only in the dark-blue theatre of our final moments,
in a flash of nostalgia and regret my guttering soul
will catch a glimpse of my stage debut – 1959: Juliet,
cloaked in an elaborate mantle of words, has a toothache.
The poor child. The eyes of Isabel and Papa
        pierce her consciousness.
From seats 1 to 24 her absent Mama fills the front row.
Her jagged nervousness pounds on the anvil of that one
        back tooth:
cautiously she chews her way through a banquet of blank verse.
Afterwards, the fit of tears between the hugs and flowers.
Moist looks from Papa and Isabel. What am I,
        some kind of onion?
Appealing, but how deep does it go? Stripped by thousands
        of eyes,
        I feel empty at my core...
Of course, I got used to it all in time: new old selves,
        stage fright,
the requisite dose of creative hysteria at rehearsals, the bus
        to God knows where...
I got used to it all and, after that jittery first year, I loved it too.
I literally lived in the theatre, obsessed by the woman
whose turn it was to borrow my body: Ophelia, Blanche,
        and all the rest.
And often enough I took the theatre home to stay the night.
        Big names as well, I admit it:
I was all too happy to share my bed with a minotaur,
a *monstre sacré*. Why? Because I was a bizarre mixture
of lasciviousness and self-doubt? Perhaps. And yet:

even then I made love (once liberated from my initial fears)
with abandon, aroused by the anonymous divinity
        that is the public.
Because the public is faceless, and my true lover.
      Love.
      Love, but
my love life took a strange turn...

We had a premiere. Chekhov's *Cherry Orchard*,
I was playing Anya and my last words were: 'Farewell,
      old house! Farewell, old life!'
Success. Champagne. And then, still sticky from the kisses,
      doubly alone
in our dressing room: Anya took off my make-up, sloshing
      from her half a glass...
'Too drunk for words, our Anya. Farewell, fair...
Good night, mirror! Good night, light bulbs!
You're just...a dazzling ellipsis for a line...
      I seem to have forgotten...'
Then I saw them. Twelve white roses, a dozen
      diffident declarations of love.
'Your passionate admirer,' whispered the card in the folds
      of loudly rustling tissue paper.
Was it the somewhat paradoxical colour? Either way,
it sobered me up at once, then got me drunk again:
a Secret Admirer was sending me flowers! Worthy of Dietrich,
      and confusing,
the thought that the auditorium's abstract black body
could become a man, with two eyes, two balls, a heart...
      For twelve long days
I received roses from my great unknown, but each bouquet
had one less white and one more red. Then he knocked.
A good six foot of gentleman standing on the threshold:
tailored suit, aftershave, panache concealing awkwardness.
His horn-rimmed glasses latched onto the patches of red
      blossoming at both dressing tables
while a smile tested the corners of his mouth:

'Close up you're even prettier than I thought...'
Everything in the room reflected my cheeks
          during this introduction.
Thomas. Nudging thirty at the time. A businessman,
          but guileless as Unrath.
He could speak my name, but no, the word's too weak –
          he could breathe it,
so that all my down stood up on end. That kind of man. Still is.
I see our very first dinner before me: our untouched plates,
          a halo of asparagus
arranged around the meat. The waiter insists on lighting a candle
and kindles (oh romantic image) a cool fire in my hair.
Thomas raises a sparkling toast to me...
I want to make him happy, I think. Explicitly.
My wild, blonde intuition. And my face flambé.

          To keep it short:
we married. Dietrich did as well, and just as young.
The jewel in my dower was the lacklustre fact
that Mama tolerated Thomas (over the phone a moment's hope
of me becoming a lady after all; but groundless, and
          soon enough
the two of them were separated by the twin walls
          of their politeness).
One of my best roles, the bride. The jubilant organ announces
          my arrival:
I rustle through the church like an immaculate illusion.
The virginal pose before the altar. The cold and shining ring
          Thomas worms onto my finger
(never suspecting that I'll lose it in the twinkling of an eye).
Yes, I'm as white as his roses. And five months gone.
And so I became the mother of my accidental daughter.
Me, a mother! It seems like yesterday. It was yesterday,
but now, today, I want to act. I need to act, and my need
is holier than the innocence of my Marina.
'By the way, they want my face on TV... Thomas?' The cat
          on his lap like porcelain.

He's reading ('Uh-huh') the afternoon paper. The yellow sunset
deforms my ardour, it makes my deepest passion over
       as domestic bliss.
Suddenly a prisoner in his sedated suburb, I start to rage
 and smash a vase (an heirloom) to smithereens...
His scarcely surprised smile. 'But, Coco!
We can get some help in for the child, can't we? Actress!'
A week later rehearsals had already started. Theatre.
       And television.
Papa's enthusiasm knew no bounds when I appeared close-up
       before him on his brand-new set.
(He rang up: 'Like an enormous magnifying glass through which
my daughter appears before me like a queen on a mint stamp!')
Thomas stayed Thomas, delighted but restrained:
an effective antidote for acute attacks of vanity
brought on by being recognised at the supermarket checkout.
But Mama's toilsome pride! It was open season on her feelings
and fate was out there gunning with a double-barrelled shotgun:
first the shock of my pregnancy, now this...
And how was she supposed to hide her love for
       her granddaughter?
       One, two, three:
the years did what years do; I acted while Marina grew.
And Thomas was always there for her! Four, five, six:
on rare nights off, I tucked her in myself, told her a story about
       a princess,
pressed stuffed animals into her open arms, kissed her
       nighty-night...
And she was crazy about the theatre! Hand in hand
       with her father
to a place of red plush: like a chocolate nestled in
       her cosy gilded box.
Lights out. Her mother in the distance. And once,
her tinny voice above a death scene, 'Is Mama ill?'

Now, in the brief timelessness of the theatre,
now, in the midst of a dream I dream out loud –

I want to say something simple, as simple as the poetry
         of pop music,
and I can't. My... our lives are so horribly intricate
we have no choice, but lie to avoid lying... We have no feelings,
feelings have us... Bah! Reason unravels in my mouth
like rope: I'm stuttering gibberish. What I mean to say
is that I loved Thomas and cheated on him all the same.
With myself. With my leading men. Good, dear, poor Thomas!
He wore his horns like a tame bull.
         'Most women have sex
with their mirrors,' said Dietrich. (If it was Dietrich.)
So what's new? We look in the mirror until it satisfies us:
our cold adultery with glass is safe: and even when the wrinkles
         come,
self-love is blind. Why did I cheat on Thomas
         with my mirror men?
I don't know. Love is a labyrinth
in which thoughts are dead ends. I know it's not always easy
         to stop acting
and sometimes it's impossible *to act*...
         Take Coco
as Desdemona in *Othello*. A three-hundred-line denouement.
Having been murdered some time ago, I lay on the bed:
as dead and patient as I ever want to be. Then, finally,
my black Venetian spoke his final words:

         'I kiss'd thee ere I kill'd thee; no way but this,
         Killing myself to die upon a kiss.'

He kissed me. Died. Fell – for me and on me,
and got Desdemona's ring full in the balls,
a prop with a stone as big as an egg... The
         much-too-yellow teeth
in that blackened face: he groaned like a dog
dreaming uneasily of cats. Carefully ('No, don't, don't...')
I turned my hand around, but the most helpless
part of him had already jumped to attention

81

for a standing ovation. Curtain. A deep red curtain:
a glowing second long, perhaps, I saw a wall of roses.
'And then?' My daughter would demand. 'Blithe polygamy?
Because sorry to say so, but Mama, you were never there
       for me.'
Marina. Means no offence. Loves her father:
'And never got pregnant again. Gosh. How did you
       manage that?
And while we're on the subject, I am Papa's, aren't I?'
       A social conscience.
A somewhat tiresome moralism. A bitter wit:
       'When exactly do you get to poly, Mother?'
(A comment worthy of Marlene's daughter,
whose 800 pages of memoirs were already familiar to me
before I was consumed by my documentary. That book!
An extra headstone, in which with blunted love she carved
       MARLENE DIETRICH BY HER DAUGHTER.
The title. And what does the myth do? Dripping with diamonds
Dietrich encounters yet another celebrity. She turns the key
and winds up the mechanism that makes the honey:
now she's got another doll that really fucks...
His gibbering love letters full of things like: 'I swear you have
       drugged and intoxicated my brain...'
But she gets bored: away with him. Next.
One day, ninety and alone, she dies in Paris...)
       But I'm not Dietrich, am I?
Thomas, Marina, I'm not Dietrich! I don't want to die
in Paris. I'm scared to death of loneliness.
Scared no appeal will get me off those ninety years.
       What's got into me all of a sudden?
Thomas! I call you and your name sounds hypocritical.
THOMAS! Are you still there? You're still there. Not knowing
what it's like to be me. I don't know myself. Strange.
I've looked into those brown eyes for thirty-five years
       and they've just given me
that old, funny feeling of swimming in baby shit.
I'm still here, Thomas. I was never unfaithful to you.

Not really.

So there I was, in that hotel... We were doing a Chekhov
(The Seagull) for our cousins up north and I was alone.
An Indian summer night. So hot the fridge just kept on rattling.
End of documentary: Coco ices the TV and pours herself
          a shot of Four Roses.
Cheers. But at four revs per second the buzzing fan
kept decapitating her shadow and the walls were too pushy.
There wasn't a single man there in her twin beds:
an empty frame for a double portrait... My head melted.
Dietrich. What did the poor woman say? 'I have been
photographed to death...' And this over-immortalised
          invisible woman
didn't even dare to face up to her own aged movies...
Alone on my ambivalent bed: Coco still wanted to be loved
and Coco still wanted to be seen by an audience
and caressed by the winking eye of a camera,
and what was love if not a divine way of being seen?
One more splash of whisky, one last cigarette —
the fan is going mad, but the blue scraps of my text
blossom on the ceiling like long-stemmed roses:

'I never think about old age, I never think about death. What will be,
will be... Then again, my dear, I'm as careful about my appearance as
an Englishman. I always keep myself firmly in hand. My dress, my hair
— always *comme il faut*... If I've kept my looks it's because I've never let
myself go the way some women do... There you are, you see — spry as a
kitten. I could play a girl of fifteen still.'

I said all these things to my audience in *The Seagull*,
I, the mature actress Arkadina... But drunk with my role
I fell asleep and dreamt difficult dreams about my mother
(who was bursting with swollen wormy veins and said:
          'Who do you think you are?')

III

Thomas lights forty candles
and holds forth in the burning gloom:
'It's not time that flies, Coco, you fly...'
And when I turn fifty he recycles the lie,
infatuated with winged words
and drunk on our Veronese holiday;
July hangs an exorbitant moon
above our ocean-going balcony,
but my blood is slow and thick
and I'm stifled in my summer frock
(as if I've swallowed myself alive)
and far away in my home town
I hear my mother's constant carping
about the change of life... I jump
at the sight of his white suit
breaking free of the night's embrace;
his *eau de toilette* gives me a kiss;
under the thin linen of his trousers
there's no mistaking his forlorn arousal.
'Ah, sweetheart,' I say, a little too quietly.
I'm flying alright. Like a fat hen.
                                    Later,
five years later, tranquillity:
my blood flows differently, but flows,
thank God, because that viscous sludge
clogging the drains of God's own temple
made me desperate. And bloated,
without putting on a pound:
like being pregnant with myself...
Touching on the subject, my memory
revisits Isabel, one momentous
afternoon. Plagued by rheumatism,
she's moved to an old people's flat,
two trams away from my suburb.

Instead of calling to say I'll call,
I go. And catch myself unawares...
What mocking coincidence makes *him*
of all people open the door
forty years after the fact? Philippe.
Not at my wedding. Not anywhere. Here.
Plaster of Paris smile. Greyed. Those eyes!
Embarrassment explodes like a fart
in a confessional: stumbling
over words and time, blushing
as if we're rusting to the spot, hardly
a day older than we were back then...
Unmistakably each other. Philippe. Me.
And this stiff, beaming Isabel
residing in an over-cleaned,
prefabricated flat is Isabel:
'So, sweetie, your double-glazed aunt
has taken a seat in the devil's waiting room!
What'll it be? Red wine? Whisky?'
Followed by a sweet cacophony
full of the old days, but with
an ever-increasing dose of now – and suddenly
I hear (cutting through the pious lies
of CNN, cutting through Saddam Hussein
on the dressing table, praying for blood
in his square khaki desert), I hear my voice,
I hear my voice that just won't stop
about the stammering machine
and woman known as Coco...
and I hear Philippe's phobias:
how pushing sixty he sometimes
lies awake in the dark for hours, how
sometimes it's not until day
has dawned in his bedroom window
like a yawning guillotine,
that his thinking rolls away...
Silence drinks wine after this antiphony.

Truth speaks in Isabel:
'Life is shit with icing,
and we eat it like there's no tomorrow.
Merde... Don't pardon my French.
Children, the trick is to eat
shit with gusto... One more
to break the habit of life?' Old age,
thinks that blonde head of mine. Old age,
thinks the reeling blonde head
I leave behind in the taxi
when I get home.
                          The next day
my mirror shatters. Facelift, facelift,
nags the splitting in my head...
After three aspirins, Coco retraces
the line of thought born yesterday
and rings up a doctor. (I'm perfectly
aware of how grotesque it is.
Vanity, all vanity. Unquote.)
Look at my face. Study my wrinkles
in the silvery water, and know:
it is the wind, the ancient wind
caressing my face. It is nothing.
'More than one hundred thousand
buried alive by bulldozers,'
says my nonchalant newspaper.
Oh, every grain of Arabian sand
that fell in the speechless throat
of one of these is greater...
I know. God of my mother, have mercy
on their souls...) Behind Thomas's back,
I go in for three appointments. A sharp
needle sups my blood: my blood is good.
The plastic surgeon's half-glasses
scan the hieroglyphics of my skin
carefully. 'I leave no traces
when smoothing women's faces,'

he says in desiccated Latin.
He does a sketch: I'll be
a balloon with a twisted frown
and a knot behind the ears... *Goodness*,
smirks the mirror. And the water
trails veins of hair and gleams
and I'm floating like a stone.
And the mirror is reconciled.
I immediately want to confess
to Thomas. 'Thomas,' I say.
His newspaper sags, the cat stirs.
He smiles at thin air.
                         The question
isn't who I am. The question isn't
who Coco is. Who do we think we are?
This little life of mine is like an island:
I sometimes hear a muffled tolling
of bells, like the big brass bells
of a drowned cathedral,
sounding up from the blue depths
that surround me... I'm raving, ranting nonsense.
What do I say in my fin-de-siècle,
what should I say?
                         Damned Dietrich
told the story in my hotel
of auditioning for the part of Lola
before von Sternberg *selber*:
he wanted her to sing a song,
seated on a piano, the charming shears
of her legs slightly open
(I guess because one never knows
when a blossoming man
might need pruning like a rose).
But our Marlene didn't have a song...
Hmmm. Couldn't she just sing something
or other that's popular in Berlin?
And so she sang *Warum denn weinen,*

wenn man auseinander geht? and became Lola,
Lola singing 'Why should we cry, when we say goodbye...'
And me? Have I got a song for myself?
Do I long for myself? I've been hedging
for more than an hour about myself!
Countless women look for themselves,
countless people look for themselves
and don't find anyone: no one's there
for them, nobody who could be them.
But if there's no Self, that's as much
as to say that the God of the self
isn't tucked away somewhere
around a corner of time: nothing
beyond my own calm insecurity
forces me into thinking that I,
like Frankenstein's monster,
am made up of bits of other people.
Because I can't just be myself,
full as I am of Chekhov, Eliot
and Thomas, full of Shakespeare
and my mother... They jabber and sing
inside me, the dead and the living,
with their relentless voices:
*You're not just your own,
we're not just our own...*

Later. One evening. I've just got back
from acting when the rain comes,
when the east wind's angry fingers
start to fidget at the house, when
the gutless telephone emerges

from its ambush – I haven't had time
to take off my coat and suddenly
that old accent's in the room, upsetting me
even before it's had a chance
to say a terrible thing about my father:
before it says anything it draws me

out of our lukewarm living room,
the way the sea sucks its victims from
somewhere to nowhere... And then
in the person of our old doctor
(eighty, but he still does my parents),
as solemn and breathless as
the dialect itself... For Christ's sake,
spit it out!... And after an enormous second,
Papa didn't feel a thing.
I will. Right away. Yes. Car. God.
And Death, who's only a rumour
when we're sixteen, is me,
standing before the window the wind
is tugging at in such a foul mood;
with the bone of a telephone in my hand
I stand there as if I've slain
my foe with the jawbone of an ass.
And I flee before death to Thomas,
to face death. I wake Thomas:
he comforts me, although I'm not crying.
Hurriedly dresses, calls Marina.
Resuscitates the car: buffeting squalls
and a monstrous downpour urge
our sedan on through the mythology
of a night that boils the heavens
through the long provincial miles
that bring me finally to Mama,
whose tears I have to dry... Wind!
be still, because my town has begun,
and the veil of morning is rent...
A young black coat at the door.
My mother, dosed-up and deaf to the world
at the kitchen table: she flinches
from Coco's kiss. Remnants of make-up
visible on her cheeks
like a yellow bourgeois mould.
Someone puts on coffee,

and the crack in my teacup opens
a lane to the land of the dead.
The clock is squared.
and upstairs someone's doing something.
Someone, an endless someone,
plays the role of the undertaker
in the unreal atmosphere of my parental home:
'Your father is laid out in the bedroom...'
He leads the way and we climb the stairs
with this moment rising before us
like a monument. Papa is ready
in the bedroom. It's been almost fifty years
and nothing here has changed. He's ready
in the cold comfort of a coffin
with clamorous fittings, even deader
than before. And more distinguished
than he was. A pinstripe suit. On display
like a bottle of spirits or a fountain pen
in the duty free: the finishing touch,
a Windsor knot that's not his style.
Thank God the priest has lit a candle:
I feel a strange, anticlerical gratitude.
They leave me alone with him.
And a quivering sarcasm appears
on his lips, his pasted hair
begins to slowly rise: and only now,
after marriage, a daughter, a war, a watch
of gold for counting other people's money,
only now does the anarchy of Belgium
rear its head on his. A hot tear
dangles from the candle. *Jesus...*
I don't have any lines for him,
the only lines I have I need
to pick out of the dust trap
of my Our Father: 'Our Father...'
Coco subjects her childhood to a snap test.
(Downstairs the new widow's head is spinning

like a prayer wheel: '...his fist
clenched, those stamp tweezers of his
wedged in that angry hand...')

And now. Mama. Across acres of car parks
the province comes streaming in
to the hospital's scattered dice.
Fretful neon inside and out.
Reception a sterilised cliché.
Trying to keep up with the doctors' gestures
and their blank, flapping coats.
The facts as bald as if
they're having radiotherapy. Here,
for weeks, I've tried to learn to talk
with her dying eighty-four years.
So full of cancer she's choking on it.
Here I sit, by her deathbed. She's wearing
the clothes they wore to sleep in an antiquity
I was part of: she's been put to bed
in an iron boat for the dead:
the chain creaks, her fingers claw
at a bank where neither grass
nor reeds can grow, the torched bank
of a youth *entre deux guerres*...
Sometimes she wheezes and holds her bones together.
Sometimes she makes a dramatic gesture
at the crucifix beyond her feet
and chews angrily at the coin
she keeps under her tongue.
She's crystal clear.
     Here I sit,
by your deathbed. With what's left of a smile
you say in your best Flemish: 'Coco?
There were so many times I was jealous...
Do you mind?' I have to speak
to come to terms with the past
and give it a new significance.

I have to tell her I don't mind.
Explain that for someone like me
there are only two possibilities:
fame or the cloister, to be loved
or to love... How can I do that?
Say it! groans the squirming
pink ceramic Jesus, who was nailed
to that cross some time in the sixties.
And I lie as honestly as I can.
And flying over the waste container,
the white smudge of a seagull
embraces us briefly
in the reflection of your window.
And Death is an agreeable man
in a trench coat sitting opposite
in the train: we've got time
for a journey abroad,
and the pensive man stuffs his pipe
and we witness the fire
he sucks into his tobacco,
and he lights our cigarettes too,
and a weird kind of speech
with a life of its own
is on our wavering lips
and the stubborn blue weed
of homesickness blossoms
on the compartment windows and grows
rampant in the depths of the night –
our lives are a transparent dream
in the last train from Bruges
to Bruges... We've got time,
Mama, we've got time.

                      What's
the rotting plum of your mouth
mumbling now?
'I have to tell you, your papa
and I... we were never happy.'

The light throbs. The room goes pale.
Oh dumb earthenware Saviour,
take pity on that purple skin,
that rotting fruit, the helplessness
with which Mama tries to confess,
and give me a cigarette. Deliver me
and give me a cigarette. I stutter.
I've given up. Cigarette. Cigarette.
Coco, that's not hospital talk.
Tortured divinity, I need a smoke.
Dying mother, I need a smoke.
Tais-toi, mon enfant. Ta gueule.
Ta gueu-ueule. Ta. Ta...

         Mama,
sometimes I appear in your theatre.
A chair. A bed. ARKADINA (*trembling*):
'No, no... I'm a woman like any other –
you can't speak to me so...'

         Again.
A chair. A bed. Mother and daughter,
another scene, another play,
but still the same. Dying light
catching your sheets. The golden window
suggesting an earlier world
that never existed. You're good
tonight, but that's relative:
'Coco, do you remember Lieve?
My ring was stolen. You were seven.
I found it under your clothes,
but kept quiet. Good riddance, I thought.
The cracks in those fingers of hers!
Worse than winter carrots.
That ring. I've still got it. An heirloom
from my mother, from her mother. Gold
with a diamond. Never wore it any more
Asleep in a drawer in my dressing table.
Soon the rest of me will be dead too.

Make sure you wear it, to stop the darkness
from smothering the stone. You stole my heart.
And after you, Marina. And after her…'
A doctor enters the room
a glorified bit player, without a prince
or secret lover to write a letter
for him to deliver. He checks his watch.
Exits. The window darkens,
becomes a blackboard. I stole from you,
but I never dared to pluck
the apple in your eye,
the apple in any other eye.
I never dared. I'm seen,
I'm seen, my heart bleeds
in my bosom. I'm seen,
therefore I'm loved. *Ah, mon enfant!*
Coco has to go. The train, Mama.
Warum denn weinen? Ta-ta. Ta-ta…

Last night I dreamt of Dietrich,
enthroned in the depths of a ballroom
and awash with the submarine blue
of old celluloid. Her face appeared
on an enormous, monstrous screen.
She shrugged and I felt scared.
Were you that woman? Your wheelchair
turned and turned and turned
on its flat tyres to face me. 'Madam,
there are maggots crawling from your legs…'
Her grin rang out demonically.
But as my hand snuffed out the alarm,
a surprised quote in my brain remembered:
'We keep on acting until Death collects us.'
Soon my palate will turn black.
(I feel a burning. Someone keeps quiet
even though it hurts. Someone whispers
that I was the most beautiful nun

in the Congo and they're right.
The clock shatters. I tear out my heart
and throw it away through the mirror.
I've never died in my life before.
I don't think I'll go to my funeral.)

I grow old, I grow old,
it's true:
seven thousand years
just leave me cold.

Warum denn weinen, wenn man auseinander geht?
Why cry?
Why should we?
Why should we?

Why?

Notes

A Public Woman includes quotes (incomplete and largely
mutilated) from the work of Auden, Apollinaire, Claus,
De Coninck, Eliot, Fellini, Nijhoff, Nolens and Transströmer.
Coco is an actress, after all, a thief of words. Yes, she has even
stolen the lines she needs from poems by Benno Barnard...
'all vanity. Unquote.'

The text also includes nine verbatim quotes, these are placed in
quotation marks. Brief acknowledgements.
T.S. Eliot, *Murder in the Cathedral* [*page 60*]
Ida Gerhardt, *Collected Poems* [*page 62*]
William Shakespeare, *The Tempest* [*page 75*]
Chekhov's *Cherry Orchard*, quoted in Michael Frayn's translation [*page 78*]
William Shakespeare, *Othello* [*page 81*]
Chekhov's *Seagull*, again quoted in Michael Frayn's translation [*page 83*]
Kurt Schwitters, *obiter dictum* [*page 94*]

The 'German documentary' is *Marlene*, a biographical film by
Maximilian Schell, dating from 1984.
The love letter Coco refers to is also real. It was written by
John Gilbert, one of the many Hollywood actors under
Dietrich's spell in the thirties. Maria Riva quotes Gilbert more
than once in her superior gossip biography *Marlene Dietrich* (1993).

EYEWEAR PUBLISHING